Caring for Your
Horse

Michelle Lomberg

Weigl Publishers Inc.

Project Coordinator
Heather C. Hudak

Design and Layout
Warren Clark
Katherine Phillips

Copy Editor
Tina Schwartzenberger

Photo Research
Tracey Carruthers

Published by Weigl Publishers Inc.
350 5th Avenue, Suite 3304, PMB 6G
New York, NY 10118-0069 USA
Web site: www.weigl.com

Library of Congress Cataloging-in-Publication Data

Lomberg, Michelle.
  Caring for your horse / Michelle Lomberg.
     v. cm. -- (Caring for your pet)
Contents: Horse care -- Pet profiles -- Horse history -- Life cycle --
Picking your pet -- Horse supplies -- Feeding a horse -- Getting to know
your horse -- Grooming -- Healthy and happy -- Understanding your horse
-- Horse tales -- Pet puzzlers -- Frequently asked questions -- More
information.
  ISBN 1-59036-117-2 (Library Bound : alk. paper)
 1. Horses--Juvenile literature. [1. Horses. 2. Pets.] I. Title. II.
Caring for your pet (Mankato, Minn.)
  SF302.L65 2004
  636.1--dc21

                                    2003001384

                    Printed in the United States of America
                    1 2 3 4 5 6 7 8 9 0   07 06 05 04 03

Locate the horse hoof prints throughout the book to find useful tips on caring for your pet.

Photograph and Text Credits
Every reasonable effort has been made to trace ownership and to obtain permission to reprint
copyright material. The publishers would be pleased to have any errors or omissions brought
to their attention so that they may be corrected in subsequent printings.

Cover: horse portrait (Corel Corporation); **Norvia Behling/Behling and Johnson**: pages 3, 4,
5, 6 right, 7 middle, 7 right, 18/19, 23; **Comstock, Inc.**: pages 20, 25 bottom; **Corel
Corporation**: title page, pages 6 left, 9, 12, 14, 15 bottom, 17 top, 24, 28, 31; **Digital Stock
Corporation**: page 17 bottom; **Daniel Johnson/Behling and Johnson**: pages 6 middle, 7
left, 10 top, 10 bottom, 11 top, 11 bottom, 13, 15 top, 21 top; **Paulette Johnson/Behling
and Johnson**: pages 16, 25 top, 30; **Photofest**: pages 26, 27; **Photos.com**: page 21 bottom;
Pictures.Net: page 22; **Royal Tyrell Museum/Alberta Community Development**: page 8.

Contents

Horses and Humans

Horses are strong and graceful. For thousands of years, horses have been trusted companions. They are hardworking and intelligent. They can also be playful and affectionate. Horses make great pets, but they have many other uses, too. Horses have pulled plows and carriages. They have carried soldiers, jockeys, and pleasure riders. Horses have been an important part of history and they are still a big part of many lives.

There are many organizations that help young people learn proper horse care.

Fascinating Facts

- George Washington owned the first Arabian horse in the United States.
- Napoleon Bonaparte was the leader of France in the 1800s. His favorite horse was Marengo, a gray Arabian **stallion**.
- Alexander the Great, King of Macedonia, rode a stallion named Bucephalus. When Bucephalus died, Alexander the Great built a city in his honor.

Horse owners must be as hardworking, reliable, and willing to learn as their horses. Horses require a great deal of care. They require food and water. They must be groomed, and their shelter must be kept clean. Horses need regular care from a **veterinarian** and a **farrier**. They also need to exercise both their body and their mind.

A responsible horse owner will be rewarded with a special partnership. A well-cared-for horse can be a reliable mount, a steady worker, and a trusted friend.

Watch out for sharp objects such as nails, glass, and wire. These objects can seriously injure a horse.

Horse owners gain their pet's trust by being responsible.

Pet Profiles

There are many factors a person must consider before selecting a horse. You should consider your age, size, and riding experience. Owners should also think about what kind of activities the horse will be doing. Will he be carrying a saddle or pulling a buggy? Will you be spending more time in the backyard **paddock** or the show arena?

APPALOOSA

- Bred by the Nez Perce Indians of the Northwestern U.S.
- **Versatile** riding horse
- Gentle and intelligent
- 14.2 to 15.2 **hands** high
- Fine coat with a thin **mane** and tail
- Most common color is dark with a white spotted patch of hair over the **hindquarters**

ARABIAN

- The oldest living breed
- Versatile riding and driving horse; known for speed
- Highly intelligent, spirited, gentle, and loyal
- 14.2 to 15.2 hands high
- Silky coat with a flowing mane and tail
- Colors include chestnut, bay, gray, or black

MORGAN

- The first Morgan was born in Massachusetts in 1789
- Versatile riding and driving horse
- Gentle and affectionate
- 14.1 to 15.2 hands high
- Thick mane and tail
- Colors include bay, black, brown, chestnut, gray, palomino, and buckskin

Horses come in a variety of breeds, sizes, and colors. Horse colors have special names. A reddish-brown horse is called a chestnut. A brown horse with a black mane, tail, legs, and ears is called a bay. A white horse is called a gray. Palomino horses have golden coats with creamy manes and tails. Pinto horses have white and dark patches. A horse with a golden body and a black mane, ears, legs, and tail is called a buckskin.

QUARTER HORSE

- Bred by settlers in the 1800s
- Versatile riding horse that excel as a cattle horse
- Athletic and calm
- 14.3 to 16 hands high
- Fourteen recognized colors, including bay, black, chestnut, and cream
- Compact, muscular build

SHETLAND PONY

- Shetlands were used to haul coal from mines in the U.S. in the 1800s
- Versatile riding and driving pony
- Measured in inches rather than hands. Grows up to 46 inches high
- Thick coat, mane, and tail
- Colors include black, brown, chestnut, and gray

WELSH PONY

- Americans began importing Welsh Ponies from Britain in the 1880s
- Versatile riding and driving horse that is also an excellent jumper
- Up to 14.2 hands high
- Fine coat with thick mane and tail
- Colors include black, gray, bay, and cream

Horse History

Between 40 and 55 million years ago, a dog-sized animal **grazed** the leaves and shrubs of North America, Europe, and parts of Asia. This creature was *hyracotherium*, the earliest ancestor of the modern horse. The tiny hyracotherium did not have hooves. Instead, this animal had four toes on each foot.

Over time, hyracotherium gave way to a three-toed species. *Mesohippus*, *Parahippus*, and *Merychippus* were larger than hyracotherium. Like their four-toed ancestor, Mesohippus and Parahippus ate leaves instead of grass. Merychippus was the first grass-eating horse.

The term equine refers to horses, ponies, burros, donkeys, mules, hinnies, and zebras.

Hyracotherium was the size of a small dog.

Fascinating Facts

- In the 1800s, teams of Pony Express horses and riders carried mail from Missouri to California. This was a 2,000-mile journey.
- The weight a horse can move over a certain distance in 1 minute is called horsepower. The power of an engine is measured using horsepower.

Pliohippus evolved about 10 million years ago. Like Merychippus, Pliohippus had special teeth for grazing. Instead of toes, this animal had a single hoof on each leg.

Modern horses **evolved** about 1.5 million years ago. The scientific name for the modern horse is *Equus Caballus*. This name combines two Latin words for horse. Horses became extinct in North America during the last Ice Age, around 10,000 years ago. They were brought back by the Spanish explorer Hernando Cortes. He brought horses to Mexico in 1519. Today, there are more than 5 million burros, donkeys, horses, mules, and ponies in the United States.

Only about 186 **herds** of wild horses and burros still roam the United States.

Life Cycle

Horses grow from frisky foals to athletic adults in just a few years. Most horses live to be more than 20 years old. Arabian horses have the longest life span. They often live more than 30 years.

One Day

Baby horses, or foals, are born after a **gestation period** of 11 months. Foals are able to stand soon after they are born. Mares, or female horses, lick their newborns dry, and nudge them to stand. It takes a few tries before foals are able to balance on their wobbly legs.

Three Years

At 3 years of age, horses have lost the short neck, long legs, and fluffy mane and tail of their youth. They can produce offspring. Mature horses are ready for serious work. They can be trained to carry a rider or pull a buggy.

Fascinating Facts

- Mares give birth to one foal at a time. Twins are very rare.
- Like human children, foals lose their milk teeth, or baby teeth, and grow adult teeth.

Four Weeks

At 4 weeks of age, foals weigh twice as much as they did at birth. Foals spend their days playing with other foals, napping, and eating. They still drink their mother's milk, and will start to graze. Foals must spread their front legs far apart to reach the ground with their short necks.

One Year

At 1 year old, foals are called yearlings. Playful yearlings are independent of their mother. Like adult horses, yearlings eat grass, hay, and grain. Yearlings are starting to change from awkward foals to graceful adult horses.

Picking Your Pet

There are many factors to consider when selecting a pet. Horses are a big responsibility and you may need to know the kind of care they need. Here are some important questions to think about before choosing a horse as a pet.

Foals younger than 4 months should not be taken from their mothers.

What Will a Horse Cost?

Owning a horse can be very costly. If you keep your horse at home, you will need space, shelter, feed, and bedding. Many horse owners do not keep their pet at their home. Instead, they pay to board the horse at a stable. Horses need regular visits from the farrier and veterinarian. Training a horse also costs money. A young horse will probably need a professional trainer. You will also need to buy riding gear called tack and riding clothes. If you plan to ride in competitions, there will be entry fees for events.

Boarding a horse can cost between $250 and $1,000 per month.

■ A horse's stall should be cleaned at least once a day.

How Much Time Will I Need?

Being a responsible horse owner takes a great deal of time. Most of the time you spend with your horse will be fun, but there is also work to be done. If you keep your horse at home, you will need to feed him daily and clean his stall. Horses need regular grooming and exercise. Horse shows, **gymkhanas**, and other events take time, too.

How Will a Horse Affect My Family?

Check with your family to see if they can help with the cost of keeping a horse. Find out if they can help with chores like feeding and grooming the horse. If you board your horse, you will need an adult to drive you to and from the stable.

Some people are allergic to horses, dust, and hay. Before buying a pet horse, find out if anyone in your family is allergic to any of these items.

Fascinating Facts

- The shire is the largest breed of horse. Some shires are 20 hands high.
- The smallest horse is the falabella. This breed grows to be only 30 inches high.

Horse Supplies

Before bringing a pet horse home, new horse owners need some basic supplies. These items will help owners safely handle and care for their horse. In addition to food and shelter, a horse requires proper grooming tools, tack, and riding gear.

To begin, a new horse owner needs a halter and lead rope. A halter is a rope used to lead a horse in the right direction. A simple nylon halter and cotton rope will work well. The halter must fit properly and not rub against the horse's head. If the halter is too loose, the horse might slip free. The lead rope is used to guide the horse's speed and direction.

Horse owners also need an assortment of brushes to keep their horse clean. A curry comb, dandy brush, and body brush will keep the horse's coat polished. A hairbrush can be used to remove tangles from the mane and tail. One of the most important tools in the grooming kit is the hoof pick. This little tool is used to keep the horse's hooves free of any dirt and stones that may cause **lameness**.

Always wear sturdy footwear around horses. Your foot could accidentally be crushed by a horse hoof.

The English saddle is smaller and lighter than the Western saddle.

Riding a horse requires special equipment called tack. For riding, you will need a bridle and a saddle. A bridle has three main parts: the headset, reins, and bit. The headset fits over the horse's head. It must be adjusted properly so that it does not rub against the horse or harm her breathing. The bit is a metal mouthpiece that attaches to the reins. Reins are leather straps used to guide the horse. The saddle must fit both the horse and the rider. A saddle pad cushions the horse's back.

Helmets are an important piece of safety equipment that should be worn when riding a horse.

Fascinating Facts

- Mules and hinnies are hybrids. A hybrid is a cross between two species. A mule has a horse for her mother and a donkey for her father. A hinny has a donkey for her mother and a horse for her father. Hybrids cannot have babies.
- Always use warm water to wash a saddle. Cold water does not remove grease and hot water weakens the leather.

Hungry as a Horse

A proper diet will keep your horse healthy and fit. What your horse eats depends on his breed and what kind of work he does. Shetland ponies eat very little feed. A show horse or racehorse will need plenty of high-energy food. Most horses need bulk feed and concentrated feed. Bulk feed includes hay and grass. It is rich in fiber. Horses need lots of water, too. They can drink up to 13 gallons of water each day.

When feeding a horse treats, keep your hand flat and rest the food on your palm. This keeps the horse from biting your fingers.

Horses enjoy having apples as snacks.

There are different types of hay, each with their own energy sources properties. Concentrated feed is full of energy. This type of feed includes oats, pellets, and sweet feed. Eating too much concentrated feed will make a horse fat and unhealthy.

Horses at pasture may get all the nutrition they need while grazing. For horses to get a healthy mix, the pasture must have a variety of high-quality plants. It must also be large enough to support the number of animals grazing on the land. Large or hard-working pasture horses may need extra hay or concentrated feed to keep fit.

Horses will graze when at pasture, so be sure there are no poisonous plants in the field.

Fascinating Facts

- All horses have a sweet tooth. Apples and carrots are a horse's favorite treats.
- If you must change your horse's diet, do so gradually. A quick change of feed can make a horse sick.
- Some of the following plants are poisonous to horses. Keep the grazing area clear of these plants and trees: bay, bracken, deadly nightshade, foxglove, hemlock, horsetail, laburnum, oak, ragwort, rhododendron, and yew.

Hoof to Head

Horses are built for life on the plains. Their keen senses allow them to spot **predators** and avoid danger. Horses are also able to communicate with a range of sounds, postures, and movements.

A horse's thick skin does not stop it from being ticklish. Horses are especially sensitive around the **flanks** and belly. Special muscles under the skin allow horses to twitch off flies and other pests.

The tail is an extension of the horse's spine. Horses use their tails to swish flies away. Horses use their tails to express their feelings. Carried high, they show happiness. Swished rapidly up and down, they show the horse is upset or annoyed.

The main parts of the hoof are the sole, wall, frog, and coronet. The sole is hard but can still be injured. The frog is a hard, rubbery triangle on the sole. The wall and coronet are like a human fingernail and cuticle.

Horses have keen hearing. They can hear more high-pitched sounds than humans. They can also swivel their ears to hear sounds coming from all directions.

Since a horse's eyes are on the sides of his head, he is able to see in almost every direction. There are two blind spots: directly behind and directly in front of the horse. Horses do not see many colors.

By age 5, a horse has a complete set of adult teeth. A horse has twelve **incisors** and twenty-four **molars**. Stallions have four extra **canine teeth**.

When a horse nuzzles you with his upper lip by brushing his nose against you, it means he wants to be your friend. The horse's strong and sensitive muzzle is also good for opening latches and untying knots.

MORGAN STALLION

Grooming

Horses groom by rolling on the ground and then shaking off the dust. They use their lips and teeth to clean themselves and other horses.

Horse owners use a variety of tools to keep their horse's coats shining and their manes and tails flowing. Just like a human massage, a thorough grooming improves the horse's muscle tone and blood flow. It also gives the horse a healthy glow.

Begin grooming at the hooves. Use a hoof pick to remove dirt and rocks. Work from the heel of the hoof toward the toe. Check the hoof for injuries. If the horse is **shod**, make sure her shoes are firmly in place.

Use daily grooming sessions to look for cuts, lumps, swellings, and skin irritations that might need medical attention.

Each grooming session should last at least 40 minutes.

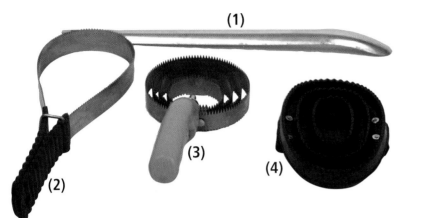

A (1) sweat scraper, (2) shedding blade, (3) metal curry comb, and (4) rubber curry comb are a few of the tools needed to groom a horse.

Next, groom the horse's body. Start with a plastic curry comb or a rubber grooming mitt. Scrub firmly, using circular strokes. Be careful around sensitive areas like the eyes, flanks, and belly. Currying raises dust and dandruff from the skin. To remove this dirt, use a dandy brush. Using firm flicking motions, work from the horse's head to her tail. For a glossy sheen, finish grooming with a body brush. Use long, firm, strokes to brush in the direction of the horse's hair.

The mane and tail should be brushed just like human hair. Use your fingers to remove big tangles and dirt. Using a hairbrush, brush from the tips to the roots.

For the finishing touch, use a damp sponge to gently clean the eyes, nose, and **dock**.

Fascinating Facts

- Some show horses wear their manes and tails in fancy braids.
- Some horse owners clip, or shave, the heavy coats of their horses. There are different patterns of clips, including the blanket clip, trace-high clip, and full clip.
- For the show ring, horses often have their hooves sanded and polished to a brilliant shine.

Healthy and Happy

Good food, exercise, and regular visits from the veterinarian and farrier will keep your horse healthy and happy throughout his long life.

Two of the most common health problems horses can have are colic and lameness. Colic is a stomachache that can be caused by a change in feed, or too much water after exercise. It can be very serious. If the horse is feverish, stretching, rolling, or looking at his belly, he may have colic. If he is restless, walk him on the lead rope until the veterinarian arrives.

Small yellow specks on a horse's hair are bot fly eggs. If a horse swallows these eggs, he may become ill. There are special products available to remove the eggs.

■ Horses should always have a supply of clean drinking water.

Farriers make horseshoes to fit a horse's hooves properly.

If your horse has an uneven **gait** when he walks or **trots**, he may have lameness. Running cold water over the sore leg may help ease the pain. Gentle exercise can also help. Check with a veterinarian first to be sure you do not harm the horse. A farrier might use special shoes to correct the problem.

Even a healthy horse needs regular medical attention. Your horse requires at least two visits from a veterinarian each year. He will need to be **dewormed** every 6 to 8 weeks. Older horses need their teeth filed once each year, too.

Proper hoof care is essential to a horse's overall health. A farrier should visit every 6 to 8 weeks to trim your horse's hooves and put on new shoes or reset old ones.

Fascinating Facts

- Veterinarians attend college for 8 years.
- Farriers hold competitions to see who is the best and fastest at putting on horseshoes.
- If you want to become a farrier, working with animals and hand tools is good practice.

Horsing Around

Horses have many ways of communicating. They use movement, posture, and facial expressions to show how they feel. A startled horse will shy, or jump sideways, from an unknown object. She will raise her head and flare her nostrils. She will point her ears forward and listen for sounds. A relaxed horse will lower her head and let one hind foot rest. An angry horse will lay her ears back. She might bare her teeth, swish her tail, or raise a hind hoof as a warning that she is upset.

A large plastic jug hanging in the stall can amuse a bored horse. Special balls are also available from tack and feed stores.

Horses lower their ears to the sides when they are relaxed or bored.

Pet Peeves

Horses do not like:
- loud noises
- bitter foods
- being startled by someone sneaking around them
- too little attention
- walking on rough surfaces
- tight halters and saddles that rub against their skin

The more you know about your horse, the better the two of you will get along. Horses do not like change. When teaching your horse a new routine, do not expect her to learn right away.

Even the calmest horse can be easily startled. Never try to sneak up on a horse. Always approach from the side, so the horse is able to see you. This will help her feel less threatened.

Horses do not like to be bored or lonely. Bored horses develop bad habits. Chewing, pawing, mane or tail rubbing, and air gulping are signs of boredom. These habits are hard to break.

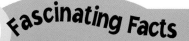 When a horse is relaxed, she may rest on her back leg.

Fascinating Facts

- Horses greet one another by blowing into each other's nostrils.
- Horses use their teeth to scratch each other's neck and **withers**.
- By standing nose to tail, two horses can swish flies away from each other's faces.

Horse Tales

Horses have delighted humans for thousands of years. There are many stories and myths about horses and horse-like creatures. In all of the stories, horses are intelligent, strong, and brave.

Greek mythology features a winged horse named Pegasus. Pegasus was tamed by a young man named Bellerophon. After many adventures on his flying horse, Bellerophon tried to ride Pegasus to Mount Olympus, the home of the gods. This made the gods angry. As punishment, Bellerophon was thrown from his horse. Pegasus went to live among the gods on Mount Olympus.

The word "nightmare" comes from Greek mythology. A horse named Aganippe punished evil people by giving them scary dreams.

Disney's 1997 movie *Hercules* featured the winged horse Pegasus.

Fascinating Facts

- The star of the 1979 movie *The Black Stallion* was Cass Olé, an Arabian stallion.
- The model for the movie *Spirit, Stallion of the Cimarron* is a real horse. The real Spirit is a breed called the kiger mustang.
- Movie and television audiences in the 1940s, 1950s, and 1960s were entertained by horses. The Lone Ranger's Silver, Roy Rogers's Trigger, and Mr. Ed are just a few of these horses.

Winged horses appear in Scandinavian mythology, too. Guided by the Sun god, Alsvidur and Arvakur pulled the Sun and the Moon across the sky. Their wings, manes, and **fetlocks** were burned by the Sun's heat. In another myth, the Norse god Odin rode a horse named Sleipnir. Sleipnir's eight legs could carry him across land, sea, and air.

In the Middle Ages, Europeans believed in unicorns. Unicorns were white, horse-like creatures that had a single horn in the centre of their forehead. People believed that this horn had magical healing properties.

In *Spirit: Stallion of the Cimarron*, a young mustang fights for freedom.

The Legend of the Trojan Horse

In Greek legend, the "Trojan Horse" is a story used to teach a valuable lesson. After 10 long years at battle with the Trojans, the Greeks came up with a plan to take over the city of Troy. The Greeks built a giant, wooden horse and filled it with soldiers. They left the horse at the gates of Troy. Believing the horse was a gift from the Greeks, the Trojans brought it inside the gates. Since the two sides had been warring for so long, the Trojans celebrated this peaceful offering. They thought it meant the end of the Trojan War. After hours of feasting, the Trojans went to sleep. As they slept, the Greek soldiers crept out of the horse and burned Troy to the ground. The moral of this story is that you should not let down your guard too easily.

From Homer's *The Iliad*.

Pet Puzzlers

What do you know about horses? If you can answer the following questions correctly, you may be ready to own a pet horse.

Q Who owned the first Arabian horse in the United States?

George Washington owned the first Arabian horse in the United States.

Q Which is taller, an Appaloosa or a Shetland pony?

An Appaloosa is taller than a Shetland pony. An Appaloosa stands 14.2 to 15.2 hands high. A Shetland pony stands 46 inches high.

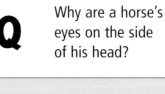

Q Why are a horse's eyes on the side of his head?

A horse's eyes are on the side of his head so that he can see in almost all directions. A horse cannot see directly behind or in front of his head.

Q What is colic?

Colic is a stomachache that can be caused by a change in feed or too much water after exercise.

Q How long does it take for a newborn foal to stand?

a) 1 hour
b) 1 week
c) 3 days
d) 1 month

a) Foals can stand within 1 hour of birth.

Q What unit is used to measure horses?

Horses are measured in hands. One hand is 4 inches. Horses are measured from the ground to the withers.

Q What does a farrier do?

A farrier trims and shoes a horse's hooves.

Hailing Your Horse

Before you buy your pet horse, write down some horse names that you like. Some names may work better for a female horse. Others may suit a male horse. Here are just a few suggestions:

Bandit

Spirit

Comet

Beauty

Prince

Rocky

Pepper

Sunny

Lucky

Silver

Frequently Asked Questions

Can my horse live in the pasture?

If there is enough space and a mix of high-energy plants, horses can live in the pasture. It is best to have two pastures so that one can grow while the other is being grazed. Pastured horses need shelter from the Sun and bad weather. They also need fresh water.

What can looking at a horse's teeth tell you?

Beginning at 2 years of age, it is possible to tell the age of a horse by the condition of his teeth. Teeth discolor and change shape as a horse ages. For example, young horses have temporary teeth that are smaller and whiter than permanent teeth. Over time a horse's front teeth change shape from round to triangular.

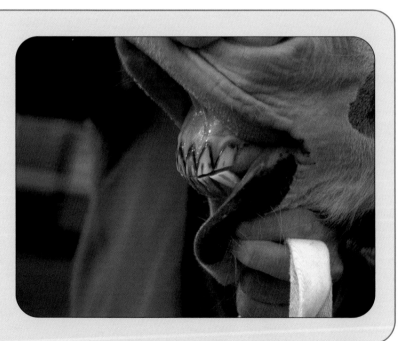

What causes a horse to become startled?

Any sudden movements, loud noises, or new colors may startle a horse. Owners should never sneak up on their horse.

More Information

Horse Organizations

You can help horses stay happy and healthy by learning more about them. Many organizations are dedicated to teaching people how to care for and protect their pet pals. For more horse information, write to the following organizations:

USA Equestrian
4047 Iron Works Parkway
Lexington, KY 40511

Certified Horsemanship Association
5318 Old Bullard Road
Tyler, TX 75703

Web Sites

To answer more of your horse questions, go online and surf to the following Web sites:

Horse Breeds
www.ansi.okstate.edu/breeds/horses

Horse Matters
www.horsematters.net

Pet Place
http://petplace.netscape.com

Words to Know

canine teeth: pointed teeth between the molars and incisors
dewormed: to be given medicine to kill worms living in the digestive tract
dock: the area under the tail
evolved: developed gradually
farrier: a person who shoes and cares for a horse's hooves
fetlocks: the joints on a horse's leg above the hoof
flanks: the areas between the belly and the hindquarters
gait: a way of moving
gestation period: the length of time a mammal is pregnant
grazed: ate grass
gymkhanas: contests of speed and agility
hands: the unit used to measure a horse; one hand equals 4 inches
herds: large groups of animals
hindquarters: the back part of a four-legged animal
incisors: front teeth for biting
lameness: soreness in one or more legs
mane: thick hair around an animal's neck
molars: back teeth that are used for grinding
paddock: a small, fenced field used for pasture or exercise
predators: animals that hunt and kill other animals for food
shod: wearing shoes
stallion: an adult male horse
trots: moves at a quick pace
versatile: able to do many things well
veterinarian: animal doctor
withers: the high point on a horse where the neck meets the body

Index